THE
REMARKABLE
BAOBAB

THE
REMARKABLE
BAOBAB

THOMAS PAKENHAM

JONATHAN BALL PUBLISHERS
JOHANNESBURG & CAPE TOWN

DEDICATION:
FOR BARBARA AND IN MEMORY OF JIM

CONTENTS

THE WOODEN ELEPHANT

TWO YEARS AGO I WROTE in the introduction to my book, *Remarkable Trees of the World*, that my encounter with an elephantine baobab in South Africa in 1996 had proved the start of a dangerous love affair with baobabs. As I said, it needed the self-control of a monk not to let them take over the whole book.

Well, now I have finally succumbed to the temptation. Here's a book bursting with ripe baobabs. Of course it's not a botanical textbook. It's a personal book like its predecessors. I have scoured the world for baobabs with shapely limbs and unusual characters. They have turned up in odd corners of several continents and numerous islands. I have seen them and fallen under their spell in Madagascar, Africa, Australia and parts of the Caribbean and Florida.

Most of the very large ones I met proved to be hollow, like old trees in Europe. Some were more like elephants than trees and slowly dying on their feet. Others were as smooth inside as a hollow gourd. I explored them as warily as an explorer climbing into a cave. You could never know what you would find. Had this giant tree been a stable, a pub, a post office or a tomb? Often the folklore was confusing.

Even more confusing was some of the scientific literature. Botanists, anxious for botanical correctness, frequently change the names of our favourite trees. The baobab has had to suffer changes in both the number and names of its species. Somehow it has survived the identity crises. At present there appears to be grudging agreement that there are eight species of the baobab genus, *Adansonia*. Six of these species are in Madagascar (three of which I have not myself seen), one in Australia and one in the whole of Africa.

The African baobab, *Adansonia digitata*, was the first to be discovered and

PAGE 2: Baobabs at Morondava, Madagascar; PAGES 4–5: Thomas Baines sketching.
PAGES 6–7: Painting by Thomas Baines, 'Figures Painted on a Rock and Carved on a Gouty Stem Tree'.

is by far the commonest. It is found in 31 African countries – in fact in every part of the African savannah where the climate is hot and dry and most other plants (and people) find it difficult to live. This is the miracle that the baobab performs. It's like the salamander that revels in the fire. The baobab puffs itself up to a gigantic size, to become one of the largest living things in the world, where other plants would wither and die.

From the beginning, the 21-year-old French explorer and naturalist who discovered it, Michel Adanson, realised this tree was the stuff legends are made of. He saw his first baobab, known to the local Wolof as the 'goui' and to the French planters as the 'calabash tree', one day in August 1749. He had paddled out to the island of Sor in Senegal, close to what is now the modern capital, Dakar. Some of the natives had taken him in a dug-out canoe to hunt antelope. But, as he described later in his book *Voyage en Senegal*, 'I laid aside all thoughts of sport, as soon as I perceived a tree of prodigious thickness, which drew my whole attention... I extended my arms, as wide as I possibly could, thirteen times, before I embraced its circumference; and for greater exactness, I measured it round with packthread, and found it to be sixty-five feet.' Later he encountered baobabs 74 feet and 77 feet in girth, and concluded: 'as Africa may boast of producing the largest of animals, viz. the ostrich and the elephant; so may it be said, not to degenerate with regard to vegetables, since it gives birth to calabash trees, that are immensely larger than any other tree now existing, at least that we know of; and probably the largest on the terrestrial globe'.

When Adanson returned to France after five years of wandering, he published a scholarly account of the tree, which was then named after him

by the great Swedish botanist, Carolus Linnaeus, alias Carl von Linné. (Adanson demurred but Linnaeus insisted.) The young explorer modestly asked why this prodigy had been missed by his predecessors. Earlier botanists had described it from the fruit, but had never seen either the flower or the tree itself. Adanson was right about the tree and its amazing properties.

We now know that the baobab's fruit was on sale in the market in Cairo as early as the 16th century, apparently brought by the slave caravans from the Sudan far to the south. But no European traveller had described the tree. In fact throughout the poorer parts of Africa the fruit was a godsend. The seeds are like small black beans and are delicious if first roasted. The white pulp which protects the seeds made a sherbet-like drink rich in vitamin C. And the outer shell, hard and waterproof, made all kinds of domestic articles from castanets to calabashes. The tree, too, was a godsend to the poor. If you needed fresh salad, you could eat both the elegant white flowers and the pale green foliage, five-lobed like a hand (hence the specific name, digitata). It is true that, rated as ordinary timber, the tree is useless. The wood is so fibrous and spongy – more like balsa than hardwood – that you can drive in a nail without a hammer. Yet the bark can be stripped from the trunk, harvested like cork from cork trees in Portugal, without killing the tree. Pound the bark and you have made a rope; weave it and you have bark-cloth to wear; flatten it and you have the tiles for your roof.

As well as describing the trees, Adanson made two striking claims: that baobabs were probably the largest and the oldest trees on the globe.

Take first their astounding size. Now Adanson lived a century before the discovery of the giants of the north-west Pacific coast: coast redwoods, giant

PAGES 10-11: Namibian Ju'hoansi men rest inside the trunk of a baobab after a hunt.
LEFT: The flower of the Australian boab with stigma ready for the kiss of the hawkmoth.

sequoias and red cedars. Measured in volume those are much bigger trees. Measured in *girth* the baobabs are the biggest – except for one single specimen of the Montezuma cypress at Tule in southern Mexico. Of course the current champions are not the 75-foot or 77-foot baobabs Adanson saw in Senegal 250 years ago. Today one is told that four separate trees in the northern lowveld of South Africa are known to have exceeded 100 feet in girth. I visited all four this year and put my tape around their Brobdignag stomachs (see pages 75–7, 78–85, 86–93, 94–7). I can confirm their astonishing credentials.

The age of baobabs is more baffling. Adanson claimed that the trees were 5,000 years old, which meant they literally went back to the Flood. No modern botanist would agree with that. Until recently it was usual to say that the largest baobabs were several thousand years old. But in the absence of annual rings to count (even if an old tree is not hollow, as it usually is, there are no dependable annual rings) the scientific evidence is tenuous. What is certain is that very large baobabs can be very young (see page 124). So most botanists now credit the oldest baobab with about the same age as the oldest oak in Europe – say, 1,000 years old.

Still, they were Methuselahs in a world where history largely passed by word of mouth. And it must be due to their great age as well as to their stupendous size – and astonishing shape – that so many legends have accumulated around them. The best-known is the African creation myth of the tree-turned-upside-down. When God made the world he gave each of the animals a tree. The hyena was given the baobab but threw it down in disgust – and the tree landed upside down. Hence its extraordinary shape.

Other traditions are more flattering, as one would expect. After all many African peoples depended on the tree for food, shelter and clothing. It was a tree like a god, benevolent but dangerous to offend. No wonder they associated it with the spirits of their ancestors, who had to be worshipped and appeased. And when a great baobab died, which occasionally happened, the tree was accorded the privilege of a solemn burial.

Seydou Drame, a West African writer, recently described the funeral rites of one of these 'wooden elephants', rites which he had witnessed:

Having a funeral for a tree might seem like something out of a fairy tale. But for the people of Kassakongo, and for the Marka (in Burkino Fasso) as a whole, it is in fact a real and living tradition. Not all trees have the right to such special treatment. The only ones are those which have played an important role in the life of the village, providing a resting place for local gods and a secret meeting place for the ancestors. A refuge for spirits, the Baobab of Kassakongo was regarded as a father: to 'his' sons 'he' gave everything...

One day its leaves failed to grow again. Still upright, the old wooden elephant had given in to death, and so it was the whole village prepared for its funeral.

In Kassakongo the chief tells the story of the Baobab's life as if he were talking about an old man who had just died. 'He chose to take up residence in Kassakongo. The villagers took his presence to be as blessing from God'. At the chief's side storytellers sing the praises of the baobab and ask for its protection... Special rhythms, normally reserved for chiefs, are played on the drums. For the tree was their benefactor. 'Was it not the Baobab who gave his leaves to enrich them in the years of want. Was it not he, again, who bent his ear to the tears of women and children and the cries of men in the time of sorrow?'

THE GREAT PROVIDER

LEFT: A young African baobab (*Adansonia digitata*) stripped of its bark by villagers. Fortunately the baobab is not injured as it can grow a new bark, like the cork oak in Europe does. The fibres of the inner bark, strong and durable, make roof coverings and bark-cloth. The bark is also used to make ropes of all kinds – for harness, fishing lines, baskets, nets and so on. In Senegal and Ethiopia it's used to make waterproof hats that also serve as drinking vessels.

CENTRE: Seed pods of the African baobab. The stalks of baobabs can be over two feet long, and hang down in clusters (giving the baobab the name of 'rat-tail tree' in the Caribbean).

RIGHT: Seed pods cut open to show the acid pith and seeds inside. Mixed with water the pith makes a refreshing drink like sherbet, and can also be used in baking as a substitute for cream of tartar, or in medicine as a replacement for quinine. The seeds are eaten raw or roasted as a substitute for coffee beans. The empty seed pods are made into cups, snuff boxes and fishing floats. If the seed pods are burnt, the ashes can be used as soap.

THEY SAILED FROM HERE

SUNSET AT THE AVENUE

ONE SUMMER DAY ABOUT FIVE YEARS AGO I found three mysterious Japanese travellers – a young man and two very beautiful girls – on my doorstep in Ireland. They had come, they said, 12,000 miles to see an ancient beech tree in our demesne. Who could resist such a charming compliment?

Unfortunately the great beech is now a ruin. I showed them the tree, its five trunks splayed out on the ground like a starfish. They took the sight with stoicism. Then I stood them all a Guinness in the local pub. Before they left, the young man, who said he was a professional photographer, gave me an astonishing postcard of some trees he had photographed at a place called Morondava in Madagascar. It was called Sunset at the Avenue of the Baobabs. Was it really a photograph? It looked more like a surreal painting. I could hardly contain my impatience to go there and see.

But it was not until two years later that I had the good fortune to be in Morondava myself. If you fly low along the hot, dry littoral on the west side of the island, you will know Morondava by the forest of baobabs which encloses the town on the north side. Some of the trees look enormous, and even from the air they appear to be a more upright and elegant shape than their African cousins. And so they are. This is *Adansonia grandidieri*, the strangest and most magnificent of all the six baobab species which are endemics, meaning they are unique to the island.

Why are there six species of baobab in Madagascar and only two in the rest of the world, 10,000 miles apart in Africa and Australia? This is the mystery of 'disjunction' that has puzzled botanists ever since this treasure trove of Malagasy baobabs was discovered by French explorers at the end of the 19th century. (The French had seized the island during the scramble

PREVIOUS PAGES, RIGHT AND THE FOLLOWING FOUR PHOTOGRAPHS:
The much-photographed Avenue of the Baobabs, Morondava, Madagascar.

for colonies in Africa. To their chagrin, they found little of value in Madagascar except wonders of nature.) The standard theory to explain the mystery, until a few years ago, was that Gondwana was the key: Gondwana, the southern supercontinent which, so scientists believe, once embraced in a single land mass what we now know as South America, Africa, India, Antarctica and Australasia. It was here in the centre of Gondwana, in what is now Madagascar, that the ancestral baobabs are thought to have evolved. Then, according to the theory of continental drift, the supercontinent broke up at least 50 million years ago, and new continents and subcontinents were formed, as the broken pieces drifted away across the oceans. Two pieces, now Africa and Australia, carried away the ancestors of two of the modern species, *Adansonia digitata* and *Adansonia gibbosa*. The ancestors of the other six species were left behind in Madagascar.

This was the theory until a few years ago. But an American taxonomist, appropriately called Dr Baum, set the cat among the pigeons in the 1990s. The dates, he explained brutally, simply didn't fit. Look at the structure of the flowers of the baobab genus, and examine their chromosomes. The genus is relatively modern, meaning it has evolved only 7 to 17 million years ago. So Gondwana, which broke up at least 50 million years ago, is just a geological red herring.

Instead, Dr Baum proposed a new theory which sounded like a leg-pull but has been accepted by most botanists – and I personally find it irresistible. The intrepid baobab ancestors sailed from Madagascar in their own seed pods several million years ago, one baobab flotilla landing in east Africa, the other in west Australia.

I myself landed prosaically at Morondava, after an hour's flight from Tana, the capital, in the summer of 2001. Morondava, like most towns built here by the French, has surrendered its colonial pretensions in the cheerful, squalid chaos of an African market town. But I found an excellent hotel, the Café Baobab, run by a delightful Frenchman, who offered to take me whale-watching in his speedboat. First things first. I wanted to see the 'sacred baobabs' described in my guidebook. And I wanted to see the famous baobab avenue at sunset.

It turned out that both groups were close to the main road to the north. I took a taxi and after an hour's drive along the potholed tarmac, through small plots of rice and mealie, found one of the sacred trees beside a banana grove. It was a goliath of a tree, and too muscular to be *Adansonia grandidieri*. It must have been the other kind of baobab that grows here to the height of a 10-storey building, *Adansonia rubrostipa*. I pushed my way through thorn bushes (no chance of a photograph unfortunately) and found some ritual offerings hidden close to the trunk: some food and some flowers. There was no sign of any worshippers. But the guidebook said the giant tree was the burial place of a local woman who had been a spirit medium and healer. Her son was a Christian and rejected the old beliefs. So the tree took on her spiritual power and people came to it to be healed.

I photographed smaller examples of *A. rubrostipa*, shorter, chunkier and more bottle-shaped, in the bush to the west of the sacred trees. You can see one on page 31. Zebu cattle with long, curved horns were grazing close by the massive trunk. The bark showed signs of recent damage, presumably by animals. Nearby was a pair of embracing trees, famous to tourists as 'Les

Baobabs Amoureux'. They looked to me like a domestic couple, a Darby and Joan of the tree world, but no worse for that.

One thing that struck me about the baobabs here (and ones I saw in other parts of the country) was that they no longer seemed to have any relevance for the ordinary Malagasy, apart from the occasional sacred tree and the trees that served as a honey-pot for tourists. This must make their conservation extremely difficult. Years ago every Malagasy village in this area would have used baobab bark to serve as a roof for their huts. The ropes and nets, too, would have been woven from bark, and fishing floats made from the hollow seed pods. The pulp in the seed pods would have made lemonade, and the seed roasted like coffee beans. Now this could all be bought in local shops. The baobabs had become an encumbrance. Young trees would not be encouraged. The removal of old trees would be only a matter of time.

Close by the embracing pair was the avenue itself, and this was indeed astounding. I drove there twice across the potholes in the next two days. I should have liked to spend a week there in this surreal stage set of polished columns and roofless vaults. (I once spent a week in Agra and every day, at dawn and sunset, took a rickshaw to pay homage to the Taj Mahal.) Sunset brings *Adansonia grandidieri* to its operatic climax. But on the first day at the avenue of the baobabs I lost the sunset to an inconsiderate bank of clouds. On the second day I nearly lost it (as I have described in *Remarkable Trees of the World*) to a very large Belgian lady who stood in my way. But she withdrew, just in time, and I captured the sunset with the one eye of my lens. Here it is (see pages 18–19) – taken on ordinary film. But am I deluding myself? Doesn't it have something of the eeriness of a painting by Salvador Dali?

LEFT: Planting rice in the flooded fields beside two
baobabs near Morondava in Madagascar.

The saddest thing about this avenue is that it's probably doomed. It's not an avenue in the sense it was planted – just a remnant of a huge forest of Grandidier's baobab that once stretched northwards from Morondava. But the species is now one of the three most endangered in the island. Subsistence farmers are desperate for land for their crops. The baobabs pay the price. I saw many freshly amputated stumps. In the photograph taken by my Japanese visitor there were two extra trees. Book your flight to Morondava now before the avenue becomes a paddy field.

OPERA BUFFA AT IFATY

Of the six unique species of *Adansonia* discovered in Madagascar, three (*A. madagascariensis*, *A. suarezansis* and *A. perrieri*) live in the north and north-west, three (*A. grandidieri*, *A. rubrostipa* and *A. za*) in the west and south.

Nothing would have delighted me more than to be able to encounter all six – but one of my family was ill and I was on borrowed time. I could only pay my respects to the group in the west and south, which are the three most accessible species.

Now it's not always the best plan to catch these rare creatures in flower. They are certainly very beautiful. Unlike the African and Australian species whose flowers are white, some of the Madagascar species have scarlet flowers. But even more exotic are the scents that the different species emit in order to attract their pollinators. Three species, called the long-tubed section, depend mainly on the kiss of the hawkmoth for pollination. To lure the hawkmoth to their lips, they smell as fragrant as Chanel. Three other

RIGHT: *Adansonia rubrostipa* near the Avenue
of the Baobabs at Morondava.

species, the short-tubed section, depend mainly on bats. And bats, apparently, must be wooed with the smell of carrion.

Fortunately, perhaps, *A. grandidieri*, which is bat-pollinated, was not in flower when I came to Morondava. It would have detracted from the ethereal beauty of the avenue if it had smelt of rotting teeth. But the other two baobabs are moth-pollinated, so their breath is as sweet as roses. Unfortunately, the books said they flowered from November to January (*A. za*) and from February to March (*A. rubrostipa*). This was August and I had missed the bus. (But what better excuse for a second foray to Madagascar?)

Two hundred miles further south along the coast beyond Morondava you find the climate drier and the soil poorer. Farmers scratch their living from rearing cattle. There are vast, empty beaches of white sand, almost impassable roads and a few happy tourists. Life is difficult for the local people – and for the baobabs. The main species here is *Adansonia za*, noted for its modest size and extraordinary variety of shapes. I was told that I would see some fine examples at the small village of Ifaty, where an enterprising local landowner has given sanctuary to some threatened baobabs. Long ago, protecting the baobabs like a shield of barbed wire, there were miles of spiny forest: fantastic thorn trees, the Didiereaceae (including the octopus tree), which are found nowhere else but in Madagascar. But most of the spiny forest has now been cut down to make more grazing for cattle, so the baobab reserve at Ifaty is all the more precious.

To get to Ifaty from my beach hotel, a couple of miles down the coast, I hired a dug-out canoe, hewn out, I think, from a tamarind, and fitted with outrigger and a small sail. It was a delightful way to travel, as the wind

PAGES 32–33: Baobabs cover the side of Mt. des Francais in Antsiranana, formerly Diégo-Suarez, northern Madagascar. LEFT AND THE FOLLOWING FOUR PHOTOGRAPHS: Specimens of *Adansonia za* in the reserve at Ifaty.

blew steadily from the south and the sea was a good deal smoother than the roads.

The Ifaty reserve cannot be much bigger than a large garden, and I enjoyed the theatrical performance. It was opera *buffa*. Outrageous baobabs frisk about the octopus trees like ham actors: they play teapots, chamber pots, milk bottles, winecoolers and water buckets. The spiny forest gives a suitably Gothic backdrop. You would not survive long in the embrace of those emaciated, octopus-like arms, fitted with thorns like witches' fingernails. I am glad I returned to the safety of my dug-out canoe before darkness fell. This was not the place for a picnic under the stars.

Next day I came back in my dug-out to photograph the baobabs in their operatic setting. Four trees, all (I was told) specimens of *Adansonia za*, especially caught my eye. The first was an uncannily clever imitation of a 30-foot-high teapot. The spout projected upwards for at least half that height. I asked one of my Malagasy guides to climb onto the spout and he obliged. You can see him in my photograph. The second was a double-trunked tree with a curious deformity. I think it may once have had a third trunk that was somehow damaged. Now it projected suggestively. The third tree was more like a milk jug. Somebody had surrounded it with a circle of small white stones. I wondered whether this was the work of a local admirer – like the stones a child will use to encircle a sandcastle on a beach. No, I decided, hardly here in the wilds at Ifaty. The tree must surely play its part in some sacred ritual. The fourth was the most alluring: a slim, bottle-shaped creature in a group of baobabs mixed with octopus trees. Some were much misshapen, like carrots or radishes. But the one

I have photographed was elegant enough to serve as a giant scent-bottle or Grecian urn.

I was also anxious to collect some of the fruits from this species of baobab. All eight species have different shaped seed pods, ranging from the long, curved African one to apple-shaped and egg-shaped ones in Madagascar. At Ifaty the egg-shaped fruit of *Adansonia za* hangs in profusion from the upper branches of the trees. I should have liked to have climbed up to pick them, but octopus trees, bristling with foot-long thorns, guarded the baobabs like the dragon guarding the golden fleece. Fortunately there was one seed pod under the trees, perhaps discarded by a squirrel or lemur. (Madagascar is paradise for lemur-lovers. Half of the world's species are found here.) I cut open the velvety seed pod with my penknife. I had read that the hard white pith, protecting the small black seeds, mixes with water to form a delicious lemonade. But it proved to be even better than I had anticipated. I swear it tasted like vintage champagne.

I looked about me. For the first time I noticed that some of the trees that I had taken for baobabs actually belonged to another species. This turned out to be another kind of tree unique to Madagascar: *Pachypodium geayi*, the Elephant's Foot. Pity the poor *Pachypodium*. He has been blessed by nature with one of the most elegant trunks imaginable. He rises to the blue sky like a turret carved from ivory, crowned (during this season) with a mane of naked branches. And he carries the absurd name of Elephant's Foot. No wonder two of the trees were behaving badly in public. I photographed two trees clasped together in a wild embrace (wilder, by far, than the famous one at Morondava) and then wondered if my film would be confiscated when I

passed through Customs on my return to Ireland. Fortunately, to search for erotic trees is not one of their priorities.

To return to the baobabs, I realized that many of the trees at Ifaty have notches cut in their trunks. These, I was told, are steps cut for the men who climb the trees to search for wild honey. Bees here, as in other parts of the world, find that the flat crown of the baobab makes an excellent place for a hive. Unfortunately, the honey collectors use fire to smoke out the bees, and the trees are sometimes burnt to the ground. But I was glad to learn that the trees are still useful. I had heard so much about the role the baobabs *used* to perform long ago: the way that the husks of the seed pods once furnished every household with cups and saucers and plates, the way that bark was made into clothes and waterproof hats, and twisted up to make the strings for musical instruments. I'm afraid that to save the baobab we will need more than nature reserves and the mixed blessings of tourist developments. The tree must continue to share the lives of ordinary people if it is to remain a wonder of the world.

OVERLEAF: Aerial view of a grove of baobabs, Madagascar.
PAGES 44–5: Silhouette of a baobab at sunset, Madagascar.

THE UPSIDE DOWN TREE

THE ELEPHANT HUNTER'S TREE

JUST OVER A HUNDRED YEARS AFTER Michel Adanson had first set eyes on the baobab in Senegal, the elephant hunter James Chapman tracked down his first elephantine baobab three thousand miles away in Bechuanaland (now Botswana).

Chapman was spending the winter shooting elephant, and other game like giraffe and rhino, in the thorn scrub on the edge of the Kalahari desert. Before dawn on July 10 1852 his caravan of about 100 horses and cattle and half a dozen ox-wagons started to trek across the dried-up salt lake, 18 miles broad, called the Ntetwe salt pan. He later described the scene: 'when in the middle of this pan, we appeared to be in the broad expanse of a calm and white ocean'. However, it was bitterly cold and the flakes of salt dust, raised by a keen wind, stung the eyes of man and beast. After reaching the further shore of the salt pan, and feasting on giraffe steak, Chapman was astounded to see a vast baobab – a 'moana' to the local Tswana – rise up out of a grove of palm trees.

'We were lost in amazement, truly, at the stupendous grandeur of this mighty monarch of the forest... The dimensions which we took with a measuring-tape proved its circumference at the base to be twenty-nine yards. It had shed all its leaves (this was winter), but bore fruit from five to nine inches long, containing inside a brittle shell seeds and fibres like the tamarind, enclosed in a white acetic powder... which mixed with water makes a very pleasant drink.'

Today, tourists can fly out to stay in a richly carpeted camp in the bush close to this behemoth, now called 'Chapman's Baobab'. I flew there myself in March 1999 astride a frail, two-seater plane piloted by a generous friend.

PREVIOUS PAGES: Baobab at Khubu Island with the salt pan stretching to the horizon.
RIGHT AND OVERLEAF: Chapman's tree, with a base 85 feet in circumference, on the edge of the Kalahari desert in Botswana.

It was a delightful, if incongruous experience. 'Jack's Camp', where we stayed two nights, was founded in 1993 by a daredevil South African called Jack Bousfield, later killed in his own plane. It's now run by his son Ralph, assisted by what the tourist brochure calls a 'lost tribe of desert desperadoes'. This is certainly not a place for ascetics. More suited, I would say, for the better class of maharajah. In an oasis of fan palms on the shore of the salt pan we ate rump steak and drank champagne. Next time, to conform more to the spirit of Chapman's trek, I shall order baobab lemonade (made with the white acetic powder he liked) and giraffe. Anyway, we saw Chapman's tree and I could understand why it astounded him.

Most large African baobabs rise from a single massive trunk, their branches tapering grotesquely like inverted roots. (Hence the story of the upside down tree.) But Chapman's tree is anything but grotesque. It's a masterpiece of natural sculpture. Six vast trunks, cupped like the fingers of a hand, converge at a base 85 feet in circumference. It reminded me of Rodin's famous sculpture of two hands, the bronze he called the 'Cathedral'.

NOT AS OLD AS THE PYRAMIDS?

Close to Chapman's tree, along the sandy track followed by hunters and missionaries alike, is a second giant, 'Green's Baobab'. Green was a friend and fellow elephant hunter who passed this way six years after Chapman. His tree is unfortunately most famous for the graffiti it has had to endure on its pink flanks. Like the beech tree in Europe, the baobab in Africa has a smooth skin – an invitation to passers-by in search of immortality.

LEFT: Green's tree, with the inscription (overleaf) 'Green's Expedition 1858' clearly carved in the smooth bark.

Green's own signature ('Green's Expedition 1858') dominates the back of the tree, and although the years have stretched the lettering the inscription is astonishingly clear. How old does this make the tree? When Michel Adanson was exploring Senegal in the 1750s he was amazed to find two trees inscribed with the names of European travellers dating back to the 15th and 16th centuries. He used the apparent fact the letters had stretched so little as evidence of the immense longevity of the species. In fact he came to believe that there were baobabs still alive that pre-dated the Flood – that is, were more than 5,000 years old.

David Livingstone, the explorer-missionary who came this way about the same time as Chapman, and saw these same baobabs, was outraged by Adanson's claim. As a man who had read and re-read the Old Testament, Livingstone refused to believe that any tree had survived the Flood. Anyway the trees did not look anything like 5,000 years old. As he put in his *Missionary Travels* of 1857, 'Though it possesses amazing vitality, it is difficult to believe that this great baby-looking bulb or tree is as old as the pyramids.' His own hunch, which he thought was confirmed when he measured rings on a dead tree, was that a gigantic baobab a hundred feet around would only be about 1,400 years old.

Looking at the limpid inscription cut 141 years earlier in the soft pink bark of Green's tree, I could understand Adanson's excitement. But modern scholars take side, more or less, with David Livingstone and his hunch. A life span of thousands of years, they say, is about the limit for even the most ancient African baobabs – just as it is for their cousins in Madagascar and Australia. I'm afraid these killjoy scholars are probably right.

PINK TREES, PINK ROCKS

AN HOUR'S FLIGHT SOUTHWARDS in our small plane, fighting a headwind that threatened at one point to blow us backwards the way we had come, brought us to the strangest and most beautiful baobabs in the whole of Botswana: the cluster at Khubu Island, the Island of Hippos.

Thomas Baines, the painter-explorer who travelled at different times with both Chapman and Livingstone, did not, I think, ever see these extraordinary creatures at Khubu. If he had, his paintings would have made this remote island famous. And where were the poet-explorers who could have described the extravagant beauty of this place?

In most of Africa, baobabs rise up from a featureless savannah of thorn and sand. In Khubu the baobabs rise up from the smooth, pink granite rocks. Their situation transcends reality. Beyond the pink rocks, as far as the eye can see, is a vast, menacing lake of salt, the Makarikari salt pan. Dry for 10 months a year, it is the largest salt pan in southern Africa. You would die if you ventured here when it becomes a quagmire after the summer rains.

But we came in winter. Our plane landed with a hiss on the shimmering flats, and I counted 30 baobabs commanding the ridge above me. Most of them took strange forms. There were slim bottles and fat bottles, all swaying like drunks. There was a vegetable market of carrots and parsnips. There was a zoo full of seals and sea lions. Some of the pink trees had adopted the shape of the pink rocks. And where was the soil to sustain them? If the African baobab is a prodigy, go to Khubu to see it in its most miraculous shape.

RIGHT AND PREVIOUS TWO PHOTOGRAPHS:
Baobabs at Khubu Island growing on the pink granite.

A HERD BY THE LIMPOPO

IN THE DRY SEASON, KIPLING'S 'green and greasy Limpopo' is a dull brown for most of the way from the Kalahari to the Indian Ocean. What gives it magic – upstaging even the elephants – are the tens of thousands of baobabs that loom out of the thorn scrub north and south of the river.

In South Africa I came on one herd of 200 of these creatures (and I believe that most baobabs live in herds) which had been partly domesticated by the genial owner of a wildlife reserve at Makulu Makete, an ex-mining executive called Peter Philip. One of his biggest baobabs had space to spare for a bedroom and bathroom for tourists. Others were part of a tourist trail in which the trees hospitably played their part. Most of these trees had the ordinary African shape – if you can call it ordinary. The massive trunk rises like a wall from the ground, then the beast raises its arms to the heavens, arms which are themselves the size of a more conventional tree.

It was near sunset when I photographed the most elephantine member of this herd, which they told me was about 70 feet in circumference. (We had a wildlife expert to accompany us, and she was, I think, dazed by the beauty of the beast. At any rate she lost all sense of direction. Fortunately I had brought a compass or we might still be wandering round there.) This giant was not all menacing. No, I would call its expression benign. Yet it was clear that the tree, like many old baobabs, had been outrageously treated by elephants. They often strip layers of bark from the lower trunk, apparently chewing the soft, spongy wood to cool their thirst in the dry season. I suspect that thirst is only part of the reason. Elephants are notoriously short-tempered and they must resent the good humour of their wooden counterparts.

LEFT AND OVERLEAF:
Peter Philip and the 70-foot tree at Makulu Makete.

Several of the oldest trees have also been outrageously treated by man. I'm not referring to the bark harvest, the African custom of stripping the bark from the lower trunk, which is like the harvest of cork from the cork oaks in Spain and Portugal. Provided it's not done too often, the tree remains healthy and quickly grows a new bark. I believe that much worse damage to old baobabs in Africa comes from their use as water reservoirs. A hollow tree, already decrepit, is excavated with machetes. During the rainy season people fill it with buckets from a nearby pool. Then a tap is inserted, and the tree becomes the village water tank.

Unfortunately baobab wood is so soft and pithy that it rots easily. Hollowed out trees are used (and abused) in every way – as bus shelters, storerooms, lavatories, prisons and even tombs. Occasionally the tree gets its revenge. I heard of a huge tree in Rhodesia in the 1950s that filled with methane gas generated by decay and blew up its occupants when one of them rashly lit a cigarette.

Earlier, in the evening sunshine, I was taken to see the 'Nagmaal Tree' (Communion Tree). I was told that a century ago the Boer farmers in the neighbourhood had no church of their own within reach. From time to time an itinerant pastor of the Dutch Reformed Church would make his rounds. Marriage services and baptisms would be performed, and communion given to local Boer families. And where better to solemnise them than under the shade of this mighty tree?

I couldn't see any sign today of the sacred role that the tree had once been assigned. But someone showed me a relic of its more profane past. There were 10 notches cut into the huge, twisted roots projecting from the

base of the trunk. The roots had once served as a hide for shooting game, and there was a story that a young man had once shot 10 kudu in one day from this very spot. Not very sporting, you will say. Like a man shooting pheasants from a church pew.

LEFT: The Nagmaal tree from where a hunter
once shot 10 kudu in one day.

BRING ON THE CLOWNS

PEOPLE OFTEN MOCK THE AFRICAN baobab for its bizarre shape, calling it grotesque, even ludicrous. This is not the way I talk myself about this noble species. But I'm prepared to agree that the African baobab has a strong sense of humour. How else to explain the wild gestures, the clownish gait and the huge, Falstaffian stomach?

Botanists have termed the baobab a 'pachycaul', meaning that its vast stomach is designed to store enough water to carry it through the long months of drought. A similar talent is shown by other big-bellied trees of the savannah, the kapok tree of South America (*Ceiba pentandra*) and the Australian bottle tree (*Brachychiton rupestris*).

To conserve energy, the branches of the baobab are made to be short and stubby, and the sparse leaves to drop early in the autumn. Sometimes the roots go in search of water hundreds of feet from the trunk. When a bushfire swallows the thorn scrub, the baobab can sit pretty behind its asbestos-like bark – or grow a new layer if needed. Its extraordinary genes make this tree the supreme survivor. Knock down a baobab – and elephants do – and back onto its feet climbs the tree, cheerfully growing a new trunk. Nothing, it seems can wipe the smile off the face of this irrepressible tree.

I was struck by the tree's clownish sense of humour one day earlier this year when I drove up a gorge in the Zoutspansperg, (the Salt Pan Mountains) just south of the

LEFT: A young baobab among the mealie fields.
OVERLEAF: 'Slurpie' – short for Olifantslurpboom, or 'Elephant Trunk Tree' at Messina.

69

Limpopo. Below us was a narrow, hidden, fertile valley where the old railway to Rhodesia and the north hacked its way through red rock, clinging to the edge of the gorge. To my surprise I spotted baobabs in the mealie fields. This is normally a tree of the wilderness, not of rich farmland (although for many years the species has been protected throughout South Africa, which means it has been illegal to cut it down). In due course I photographed one of the clean-limbed young baobabs standing incongruously among the mealie stubble. But a few hundred yards along the track we saw a very different sight: half-a-dozen baobabs had fallen about laughing. Some of them lay prone. Others seemed to have tied their arms to their legs. I can offer no explanation for their behaviour – except that playing the fool seemed to suit them admirably. The tree is one of nature's jesters.

Next day we drove down to Messina, the town nearest the Limpopo and the border with Zimbabwe. There's a small park here dedicated to a single, broken-down baobab, known affectionately as 'Slurpie'. 'Slurpie' is short for Olifantslurpboom, which means 'Elephant Trunk Tree'. The tree was once the pride of the town, celebrated by the work of the local artist, Erich Mayer. But it has been tormented by fires (Africans set fire to baobabs when smoking out bees to get their honey) and children have broken off half its trunk. Still, the tree has survived its admirers. Slurpie, I salute you.

LEFT: Clown up a gorge
in the Zoutspansberg.

THE HOEDSPRUIT GIANT
(OVERLEAF)

OF THE FOUR SOUTH AFRICAN GIANTS, the first is much the oddest and most menacing: an immense, octopus-like creature at Hoedspruit, near Glencoe. The situation is dramatic. Ten miles away across the plain, dotted with neat, European-run farms, the last spiky outrider of the Drakensberg Mountains notches the horizon. But, viewed from a few hundred yards, the Hoedspruit Giant itself is singularly unimpressive. All I could see was a small wood crouching in a hollow by a farm track. I thought I must have missed my way.

Go closer and you realise the small wood is a single tree. As I pushed my way under the pale green canopy, and my eyes adjusted to the mottled shade (for this was high summer and the tree was in full leaf), I realised that the single tree is at least 100 feet in circumference. How to describe its extraordinary shape? The main lower trunk is more like a mound than a tree. From the mound arises an octopus of trunks and branches. In fact the term octopus is too coherent for this anarchic beast. Parts of its trunk arch like the neck of a tortoise. Other parts have the nightmarish quality of a monster drawn by Blake or Fuseli. I climbed the mound and then hastily descended. This is not a tree to trifle with. It would not surprise me if its crown was as full of black mambas as Medusa's hair.

Can one explain its anarchic shape? There appear to be two kinds of bark visible in the lower trunks. One section looks centuries old, as it is grey and wrinkled like an elephant's skin. The other is smoother and pinker and younger. Did this great beast suffer a catastrophic accident centuries ago? Did it re-invent itself after a hurricane or an earthquake? The Hoedspruit Giant is as silent as the sphinx.

LEFT: Another clown in the Zoutspansberg.
OVERLEAF: The Hoedspruit baobab, one of the four South African giants.

THE DUIWELSKLOOF GIANT

I SHALL NOT DEMEAN THIS gargantuan creature – one of the two largest baobabs ever recorded – by calling it by its local name, the 'Pub Tree'. It is true that it has recently been used as a pub. There's a *braai lapa* (a barbecue pit) under its vast canopy and a pub lantern nailed into the trunk beside a small doorway. Inside, the tree glows with folksy lights. Draw up your stool, says the cheery landlord, and he offers you draught Castle beer from the barrel under the bar.

But the great tree shrugs off these suburban amenities. It has its own high-sounding name. It's the tree from Duiwelskloof, meaning the tree from Devil's Gorge or Devil's Cleft. And centuries ago the devil clearly left his mark on the tree. The gigantic trunk is cleft in two as neatly as a cloven hoof. This is not a pub where I should like to linger long after closing time.

How to describe the architecture of this grim, grey leviathan? Its two façades seem to have little connection. Looking from the east you are confronted by a single, massive trunk supported by a pair of buttresses on the right. Above, six colossal branches, dividing and sub-dividing into at least thirty more, splay out sideways to form the massive roof. This is the façade that I photographed as I approached the pub entrance to the right of the lantern, under the canopy of a small fig tree which had planted itself impudently above the doorway, in a fold of the monster's bark.

It's only when you look at the tree from the west that you realise that it takes the form of two towers joined together. From this angle each of the twin towers sprouts from a triangle at the base. Above, the roof presents the appearance of a dome about three hundred feet across. In my photograph you will see the extraordinary scale. The bench where my friends are sitting

LEFT AND FOLLOWING THREE PHOTOGRAPHS:
The tree from the Devil's Gorge, now used as a pub.

is at least ten feet long. And you will notice the incongruously pastoral setting for the leviathan: the young trees elegant in the evening light and the rim of the mountains beckoning from the south.

In the heat of the day the tree, like so many great baobabs, is home to hoards of sleeping bats. Trippers come too, from all over South Africa, to drink beer in its shade and gasp at its elephantine bulk; and their gasps are well deserved. Its branches are bigger than the trunks of most giant trees. People ask themselves whether this Duiwelskloof tree or its Sagole rival down by the Limpopo, 100 miles away, is the largest baobab in the world. On successive days I unreeled my tape around their immense stomachs, five feet from the ground, and the measurement was virtually the same: 111 feet. Neither trees are trees to argue with. So why not share the honours between them? I shall give them joint gold medals for girth.

The trouble is that I cannot put my hand on my heart and say that the Duiwelskloof Giant is one tree and not two. Tree measurers take these matters very seriously, and many would-be champions in Europe – oaks and beeches especially – are disqualified because the judges decide they are two trees not one. The facts are not always easy to come by. If two trees have grown from two seeds in the same hole, they will probably look somewhat different; if deciduous, they may break into leaf at a different time. But if they are two trunks from the same root they may fuse together and appear like a single tree. But they will be two. And of course their hopes of a medal will be doomed.

I explored the second chamber inside the Duiwelskloof Giant. I was told that it was once the home of a pair of black mambas, but they were evicted

– smoked out – when the tree became a pub. Now it's used as a cool place to store wine. And I must say the owner of the pub keeps a fine cellar. After my third glass of the best South African hock I began to see things in a rather different light. Would I like another glass? Of course. And I think I can now say, after a very full examination, that the Duiwelskloof Giant (a difficult word to pronounce after four glasses) is co-champion baobab of South Africa.

No American tree has ever girthed more than this, not even the coast redwoods and giant sequoias that, judged by volume, are the largest living things in the world. Only one individual tree to my knowledge has ever exceeded 111 feet in girth. This is the great cypress at Tule in Mexico, 190 feet in girth, a tree slowly dying from thirst. Give these South African baobabs a few more decades and their stomachs will win them the championship of the world.

THE SAGOLE GIANT

IN ALMOST EVERY RESPECT, except size, the great baobab of Sagole presents a contrast to its fellow (and rival) at Duiwelskloof. The Sagole tree is a creature of the wilderness. No whiff of the suburbs here, no bedding plants and swimming pools and rent-a-tents – nor for that matter any sign of Europeans. Two centuries of European colonisation seemed to have passed by these dusty African villages without trace. The tarmac road to the Limpopo bridge, and Zimbabwe, is only half-an-hour's drive to the west. But here the lowveld is at its hottest and drabbest. Nothing breaks the monotony of the thorn scrub except the occasional explosive moment when a large baobab breaks surface like a whale rising from the ocean.

The Sagole giant, twice the size of the next largest tree in the district, sprawls over half-an-acre of bush. In its hollow centre you can hear the rustle of a colony of mottled spinetails (a bird like a swallow). I have heard that birdwatchers travel hundreds of miles to see this colony, one of the largest in South Africa. I peered into the cave where the birds nest. A faint light shone down from a hole like a skylight 30 feet above my head. The walls were splashed with bird droppings, the floor a foot deep in them. Apart from the exotic colony of spinetails, this tree is apparently home to other birds. No doubt there are red-winged starlings and swifts as well as the ubiquitous buffalo weavers. With so many holes in its vast trunk the tree would be just the place for lovebirds and parrots. Perhaps there's even an eagle? It's the eagle that acts as the guardian of the nests of small birds, as its presence deters rats and mice and other nest-robbers.

Outside all seems confusion. How many trunks does it have, and how many branches? Indeed how can you distinguish the two? In a photograph

LEFT AND FOLLOWING THREE PHOTOGRAPHS:
The Sagole tree – is this the biggest baobab in the world?

it looks like a caricature, a cross between a beached whale and a half-deflated balloon. But if you climb its huge grey flanks, accessible from the west, you will feel something of its power. This is a veteran that still carries itself like a king. No wonder that the tribal ruler of this region, King Shivasa of Venda, came here recently in solemn procession with drummers and dancers. It was the time when astronomers had forecast that the valley of the Limpopo would be blessed with a total eclipse of the sun. And the tree, veteran of such occasions, provided the perfect viewpoint for King Shivasa and his court.

THE LEYDSDORP GIANT

BROUGHT ON A WEEKEND JAUNT by a generous publisher and his family, I first came to the Leydsdorp Giant in 1996. I took one look and the giant swept me off my feet.

It was not only the first baobab I had ever encountered. This was, I suppose, the largest tree I had seen anywhere in the world, as I had yet to meet the coast redwoods and giant sequoias of California, or the even bigger-girthed cypress of Tule, Mexico.

Of course, great size is rarely combined with great elegance – as it is in the case of that extraordinary Tule cypress. This Leydsdorp creature might be called magnificently ugly. It rises with vast, muscular arms above the dusty plain to the east of the ghost town of Leydsdorp (in what used to be known as the eastern Transvaal and is now officially Mpumalanga) In the 1880s, Leydsdorp was a boom town, as emeralds were discovered nearby and there was a gold rush to this part of the Transvaal. The Leydsdorp Giant, like the Duiwelskloof Giant, was hollowed out to make a bar. But Leydsdorp's boom soon evaporated (there was more malaria than gold and emeralds) and the town and tree were abandoned to their fate.

When I went there first nine years ago, the entrance to the bar was about a foot wide. We climbed up on the twisted roots and peered inside. The most agile of the party, my publisher's 14-year-old stepson, squeezed into the cavernous interior. It smelt of stale beer, he reported, and there were some beer cans on the floor – but no gold miners. Obviously its current role was to serve, like so many great hollow baobabs in different parts of the world, as a rubbish dump.

LEFT AND OVERLEAF: The Leydsdorp Giant. Like its rival,
the Duiwelskloof Giant, it was hollowed out to make a bar.

You would hardly recognize that tree today. I went there this March and I was delighted to find that a neighbouring farmer has appointed himself its unofficial guardian, running short courses on the spiritual life of men and trees. The Leydsdorp Giant is now, in its own way, a place of worship. The farmer has cleaned up the entrance to the old bar and made a small wooden staircase. Baobabs, even old baobabs, can grow fresh bark over their wounds very rapidly. Was it my imagination or was the entrance even smaller now today than nine years ago? My companion, a slip of a girl, squeezed with some difficulty into the belly of the tree. It's hard to believe that randy gold miners once pushed and shoved to get their beer at a bar wide enough to serve 15 men abreast. Today, my friend reported, the interior is as cool and chaste as a chapel.

In the past visitors desecrated the tree with their autographs and hammered spikes into the trunk so they could climb the tree. Nothing can be done to erase the graffiti, but the farmer has removed the spikes and built a new ladder that reaches 30 feet up the trunk. I climbed up myself and saw a friendly-looking snake sunbathing in the heat of the day.

BEHAVING BADLY TO BAOBABS

I WAS ONCE TOLD BY A MYSTIC who loved trees that inside every baobab is an elephant waiting to get out. How else to explain the elephantine limbs we see in the great trees, the legs and trunks and faces that confront us as we pay homage in their shade?

I should like to believe myself in the spiritual links between the giant tree and the giant animal. But it's well-known that when the bad years come to South Africa, and drought grips the Kruger National Park, the elephants take it out on the baobabs. Of course the leaves are part of their normal diet. But when maddened by drought they will tear off strips of spongy bark to chew. (They spit them out after extracting the salts and juices.)

Most trees would give up the ghost if the circle of delicate cambium was torn off in this way. The baobab is irrepressible: it simply grows a new circle of fleshy bark to cover the wound.

Worse, the elephant will sometimes wrench branches from the baobab and even tear the trunk from the ground. Scientists say that they are puzzled by this wanton aggression. Personally I think that the beasts resent the stoicism of the trees, and their general good humour. Elephants are notoriously short-tempered themselves. And is there a Freudian reason why they take it out on the baobabs? Do they resent the challenge of the tree as a rival elephant, just as a madman shakes his fist at his own reflection in the mirror?

Of course the same question can be put the other way round. Why does the long-suffering baobab put up with the elephant? Why indeed does it put up with all its other parasites and tormentors – the weaver-birds that disfigure its branches, the fruitbats that eat its tender young leaves, the

RIGHT AND OVERLEAF: Elephants in Kruger National Park.
Sometimes they will tear trees clean out of the ground.

baboons that chew its seed pods, the cotton bollworms and mealy bugs, the boomslangs and other venomous snakes that abuse its hospitality?

Why indeed does it put up with us? Think of the way we have massacred innocent baobabs in Africa. Thousands of great trees were drowned by the dam at Kariba. Their corpses slowly rose to the surface as the lake filled. Tens of thousands more were uprooted in west Africa because they were hosts to insect pests which plagued cotton and cocoa. (They died in vain, as the insects found other homes, and the massacre of baobabs was abandoned as a terrible mistake.)

There is one obvious answer. The tree needs us all – fruitbats to pollinate its flowers, baboons to distribute its seed pods, elephants to dump its seeds in their dung, man to plant its seedlings to give food and shade. And what a princely reward it gives us all in return!

LEFT: Bark ripped off by elephants. They chew the damp, spongy bark during a drought.

FRAGRANT FLOWERS

GO TO THE TOWN OF DERBY, if you can, when the Australian baobab (*Adansonia gibbosa*) is in flower. I did. You could have fried an egg on the pavement – the temperature was about 110 degrees – but this was paradise.

Derby, roasting in the extreme north-west corner of Australia, can claim that it's the baobab capital of the world – except that the Aussies can't pronounce the word baobab and call it 'boab'. The tin-roofed town has its streets lined with boabs, including gnarled, wild creatures that have been given the freedom of the place. I was told there's a noisy annual Boab Festival, complete with rodeo and mud crab racing. Recently a huge, ancient boab had crashed to the ground opposite Rusty's general store, and the whole town was plunged into mourning.

I had flown from Perth to Broome, a thousand-mile leap out of cool, green fields and into the flaming tropics, and then set off to drive through the empty-looking bush the last 120 miles to Derby. After an hour the first boabs appeared with mysterious abruptness. I recognised the tree, of course. Who could mistake it? Like its African counterpart, the boab dramatically rises out of a nondescript landscape of thorn scrub, rock and sand. At first sight the two species, *A. digitata* and *A. gibbosa*, look surprisingly similar. There are upside down trees here, too – trees with massive trunks and short stubby branches sticking out like roots. But there are bottle-shaped trees which seem more common here than in Africa – bottles to please an army of alcoholics, of every shape and size, from 80-foot champagne bottles to miniature bottles of crème de menthe.

It was only when I reached Derby that I realised my incredible good luck: I had stumbled into the town just when the boabs were in flower. It

RIGHT, PREVIOUS PAGES AND OVERLEAF:
Upside down trees in the Australian bush. Boabs between Broome and Derby.

was exactly like being in Kyoto in the season for cherry blossom – except it was hotter, of course, and there were fewer people about. And I must say that I found the boab's flower is even better looking than the cherry's. The petals are large, and wax-white, with a mass of white stamens and a great, long stigma – and, unlike the bat-attracting nectar of its African cousin, its own nectar smells delicious. (I can only congratulate the Australian hawkmoth, the main pollinator, for insisting on this excellent arrangement.) There's another good result of having a moth to pollinate the flower. The boab's flower proudly holds up its head to meet the embrace of the moth, while the flower of the African baobab droops to accept the kiss of the bat.

The difference in the two kinds of flower has recently helped botanists to get closer to resolving some of the many mysteries about the baobab. The genus originated millions of years ago, so botanists believe, in Madagascar. From there it spread the short distance westward to Africa. But why and how and when did it get to Australia, 6,000 miles away eastward across the Pacific, missing all the intervening tropical countries like India?

Dr David Baum, the American botanist who has delved deepest into the mysteries of baobab taxonomy, believes it sailed. Like many other seed pods carried by wind and current across the oceans, the baobab seed pod was completely watertight. Baum thinks that a seed pod of *Adansonia madagascariensis* sailed to north-west Australia from Madagascar several million years ago, either on a direct voyage, or stopping off for a time in Asia. When the first intrepid baobab landed, a local hawkmoth was conveniently waiting on the shore, eager to pollinate its flower.

One moment, Dr Baum! People tell me that the seed pod of the

Australian baobab, unlike those of the other species, is not at present watertight enough to sail across even a small pond. Ah, says Dr Baum, it's had plenty of time to adapt to its new environment. In Madagascar there were lemurs in attendance ready to open the seed pod to let the seeds germinate. Here in Australia it has evolved a self-opening seed pod: a soft, thin shell that breaks open on falling from the tree. Hey presto!

But the pods still weigh a pound or two – so don't forget your hard hat.

LEFT: Unlike its South African cousins and some of the Madagascan species, the flower of the Australian boab smells delicious.

DINNER TREE AND PRISON TREE

DERBY, THE HARBOUR BESIDE the mud flats of King's Sound, may well have been the place where the first *Adansonia madagascariensis* landed. The natural spread of the boab makes this look likely. It has pushed its empire south towards Broome, and eastwards across the Kimberley range of hills to Fitzroy Crossing and into the wilds of Northern Territory.

Today there are two famous boabs in Derby. Or perhaps I should say, one famous and the other infamous.

The celebrated Dinner Tree stands in a small group of shapely boabs on the edge of a lagoon. They tell you at the tourist office that this was where the cattle drovers stopped for their midday meal on their way to the harbour. I suppose there was once a corral beside the tree. The cattle would be watered and rested before the laborious job of loading them on board ship for the journey to the slaughterhouses of Perth. The drovers would eat their sandwiches under the shade of the Dinner Tree. It's a poetic spot – especially with boabs in flower above one's head as white as lilies in a painting by Burne-Jones. At midday the tide was out, but I saw a pair of mirages imitating the waters of the lagoon. I ate my own sandwiches there and wished I could return at dusk to watch the hawkmoths pay court to the boabs. I believe the flower petals begin to open soon after seven o'clock. The hawkmoths hover like miniature hummingbirds. Then they plunge their beaks into the fluffy white brush of the flower to suck the nectar, generously dusting the female stigma with male pollen in the process.

A few miles away, just to the east of the tarmac road to Broome, is the huge, spherical, hollow, menacing Prison Boab. According to the story they tell you in the tourist office, this is where groups of wretched Aboriginal

PREVIOUS PAGES: A boab in flower among the ant-hills near Derby.
RIGHT: The Dinner Tree on the edge of the lagoon at Derby.

prisoners, chained together like slaves, were lodged on the last stage of their journey to the court house at Derby. (If convicted, they could be sentenced to forced labour in the pearl fisheries, which was much like a death sentence.) Probably the story is true, although in daylight at least the prisoners may have been chained together in the shade of the tree rather than locked up in its cavernous interior. But strange to say there are no written records to confirm the story. One explorer who visited the tree in 1916, Herbert Basedow, looked inside the hollow trunk and found it littered with bleached human bones and a skull with a bullet hole through it. Basedow believed the Aboriginal people had once used the place as a sacred site for their dead.

I drove out to photograph the sinister tree, incongrously beautiful in the evening light. There was a token barrier around it, to protect it from autographs (too late, of course). I climbed underneath and peered into the gloomy void. I saw nothing to suggest how it had once been used, except for some empty cola cans. Prison or mortuary, house of horror or temple of mysterious rites, it now has a new role – to serve as a rubbish dump.

LEFT AND OVERLEAF: The Prison Tree at Derby
where Aboriginals were chained on their way
to be tried at the court house nearby.

A BOAB TOO FAR

I HAD READ AN ADMIRABLE BOOK on boabs, written by Pat Lowe, and I was struck by one enterprising young tree depicted in the book. Apparently originally deposited in the dung of a rock wallaby, it had seeded itself on a pinnacle of limestone in the Oscar Range near Fitzroy Crossing. Where was Fitzroy Crossing? Two hundred miles east, they told me - just a step or two away in this vast continent.

I drove there next morning with a thunderstorm blackening the sky. After four hours I turned down a dirt road and soon came to a gravel pit with boabs in flower. One had been knocked over by a truck and lay with its belly ripped open. Yet the gallant tree still flowered as if nothing had happened to it.

I reckoned I was only a few miles from Pat Lowe's enterprising tree on the pinnacle, when I came to a ford. A small river, fed by the thunderstorm, flowed across the road. Was I a man or a mouse?

I stripped to my underpants and waded across the river. It was hardly over my knees. But would the hired car stall? Equally important, was the water rising and would I get back? And who would pull me out if the car got stuck? I was quite alone and I hadn't seen a soul since I left the safety of the tarmac.

Reluctantly I turned back to Fitzroy Crossing, and next evening, leaping the Pacific in a single stride, flew to Kyoto where the cherry trees blazed in the cool, autumn sunshine.

Yes, I suppose I was a mouse.

RIGHT: A boab near Fitzroy Crossing, knocked over
by a truck but still gallantly flowering.

IN CAPTIVITY

SPOILT ROTTEN IN FLORIDA

THE WORLD IS FULL OF BAOBABS. Most are wild-sown, the seeds scattered by wind, birds or ants (or dropped in the dung of rock wallabies, lemurs or elephants). Many have been planted by man, for food or refreshment, in the hot, dry parts of the regions where they are native, in Africa, Madagascar and Australia. But many, too, were taken with African slaves to countries where both men and trees have now been given their freedom, especially the islands of the Caribbean and tropical Asia.

I have seen a liberated baobab rise up, incongruously African, beside the native banyans in the gardens of the Taj Mahal. And I believe you can't walk down a pavement in Hawaii without bumping into a plump young baobab.

Here's one of the most pampered baobabs: the young giant in the Fairchild Tropical garden in Miami. Unlike its forefathers in Africa, it can drink whenever it feels thirsty, and its branches are carefully manicured. I asked the handsome young director, Mike Maunder, when it was planted, and his answer flattened me. The tree, already 20 feet round the waist, is a mere boy in baobab terms – only 65 years old. What will the tree look like when it's 1,000? Or will it never reach that sort of age? Mike believes that in Africa, too, baobabs grow much faster than anyone realises. He's sceptical about even attributing 1,000 years to the giants. 'Perhaps 500 years is about as long as the species can live anywhere. The wood is very soft, and the trunks soon become hollow'.

I suppose Mike's depressing words apply equally to the Australian species and the baobab species native to Madagascar. We shall know – in due course – whether he's right. At the University of Arizona they have an experimental planting of some of those endangered species from Madagascar.

PREVIOUS PAGES: Not a baobab but the next best thing. The kapok or silk cotton tree (*Ceiba pentandra*) in a private garden at Palm Beach, Florida. The tree is a fellow member with the baobab of the Bombacaceae family (see also page 69). RIGHT: A pampered young tree in the Fairchild Tropical Garden. Only 65 years old, but already a giant.

THE JUMBIE TREES
OF THE CARIBBEAN

THIS MARCH I FLEW TO the delightful island of St Croix, once a tasty Danish sugar island and now a prosperous member of the US Virgin Islands. I knew little about it except that people said it had baobabs galore – more baobabs than any other island in the Caribbean. No one knows exactly why or how the species was introduced. In the 17th and 18th centuries the British and Danish planters on St Croix grew fat on African slaves and plantation sugar. When the wind blew from Senegal and Guinea, it brought shiploads of African slaves, and somehow the African baobabs came too. Clearly they were brought as seeds. But were they imported into the Caribbean by black slaves or white slave-owners?

By slaves, according to Michel Adanson. It was an African custom to carry seeds as emergency rations for a journey, and the baobab seed was a special 'treasure' like the pistachio nut and the tamarind seed. Adanson, the discoverer of the baobab, was exploring Senegal in the 1750s, when the Atlantic slave trade was in full swing. No doubt he saw the lines of shackled slaves being ferried across to the slave ships. He apparently himself witnessed the way the slaves carried baobab seeds in a small pouch slung over their shoulder when they went on a journey. But his main source about the export of baobab seeds was a fellow naturalist in Martinique, in the French West Indies. He told Adanson that there was a young baobab on Martinique which had already flowered and borne fruit. This young tree had been 'sown from seed brought by some slaves who had arrived from the coast of Africa'.

In St Croix I was given a more romantic version of Adanson's story. The slaves' descendants say their ancestors arrived with 'jumbie' necklaces around their necks – made from the seeds of 'jumbie trees' (spirit trees) back home

LEFT: Trees in Butler Bay, St Croix, the US Virgin Islands.
Baobabs are known in St Croix as 'dead rat trees'.

in Africa. Whatever way they travelled, the baobabs became the biggest-girthed trees in the Caribbean. And on St Croix, where there were over 100 trees, they served, along with the imported tamarind, as 'jumbie trees' like the mother trees in Senegal and Guinea.

The largest, and presumably oldest baobab on the island is the triple-trunked creature in the small village of Grove Place, a somewhat seedy suburb a few miles from the capital. I was taken there by one of the tree's keenest admirers, a local ethnologist, Olasee Davis. Olasee wore a white hairnet over his dreadlocks, and carried an all-purpose machete, in case we needed one. And we did.

I had read that this Grove Place tree had once been at the centre of the island's turbulent history. During a rebellion against Danish rule in 1878, the tree became first the rallying point for the insurgents and then the gallows on which the leaders were despatched. Later, the site was used for public meetings and protest marches. Eventually it became a pleasant backwater, a small park with benches, and the tree served as a public notice board – until Hurricane Hugo came roaring through the Caribbean in 1989.

Somehow the tree survived Hugo, and survived the mayhem Hugo left in his path. But I was astonished to find that today this heroic survivor is largely ignored. Once it was a jumbie tree and a symbol of suffering and resistance. Now, apart from Olasee and his friends, no one seemed to give a damn. I realised that people no longer bothered to pick up the seed pods which littered the ground. (I suppose they prefer cola to baobab lemonade.) The place was used as a rubbish dump, and the tree itself was half hidden by thorn bushes. Olasee's all-purpose machete was invaluable for cutting

RIGHT: Olasee Davis with a baobab at Butler Bay, St Croix.

down thorn bushes and removing toxic-looking cans and bottles.

Who will cut the next crop of thorns and remove the next incoming tide of cans and bottles? Fortunately a group of academics and other enthusiasts in the US Virgin Islands have started a project to publicise – and so preserve – the jumbie trees. Let me offer them my congratulations!

More inspiring than the Grove Place tree was the group of two- or three-hundred-year-old baobabs at Butler Bay, an old sugar estate a few miles down the coast. The factory buildings are abandoned and roofless. But the trees are in their prime, and look good for a few more hundred years. I came there when the branches were decorated with velvety seed pods on two-foot long stalks (hence the unromantic name for the baobab in St Croix is the 'dead rat tree'). How delightful to be there when the large, waxy, hibiscus-like, white flowers hang down from the branches.

Best of all, Olasee took me to see a 35-feet-broad baobab he had recently discovered. It was lurking in the jungle of rain-trees and liana to the east of the ruined sugar factory. We approached it gingerly, carrying the all-purpose machete in case of trouble. An hour's hacking and we could see the outline of the tree. It was a real jumbie tree – the home of ancestral spirits.

Old people on St Croix have told researchers like Olasee that when they were children they were warned not to go down to the jumbie trees at night as at the full moon the hollow would open and lead them back to Africa.

I wish I had been able to stay for the full moon, as I needed a free ride to Africa.

LEFT: The Grove Place baobab – one of the biggest in the Caribbean. Once a rallying point for rebels, sadly it is now a dump for rubbish.

THE PRISONER OF THE SUN KING

BAOBABS TAKEN INTO CAPTIVITY ARE RARE these days, thank heavens. But here's a grim example. It's a hundred-year-old creature that was dug up twenty years ago in Venda, in the northern Lowveld, and taken to grace the garden of a huge gambling complex, Sun City near the town of Krugersdorp in South Africa. This was during the days of apartheid when gambling was illegal in South Africa but not in the *bantustans* – the 'independent homelands' created as dumping grounds for surplus Africans. The then owner of Sun City, the Sun King, was the notorious Sol Kerzner.

I first saw this poor creature soon after its arrival, with a dozen fellows, in the garden at Sun City. The city looked marvellous, a Hollywood mogul's dream, complete with Temple of Doom. The tree looked terrible. In fact it looked like a man being tortured. Its main branches had been sliced off so that it could travel more easily by lorry. Its roots had obviously been mutilated too. Tubes were attached to its torso. It was a shocking sight but I didn't expect it to live long.

I came back this year and, to my surprise, it was alive and well – in a fashion. In Sun City (now re-discovered as Lost City) water flows like champagne. The prisoner is denied nothing he might fancy. Incongrously surrounded by a jungle of Malagasy plants, including the octopus tree, he has grown a foot or two in the twenty years he has been here. But he still looks like a man tormented. There are new owners these days presiding over the Temple of Doom and I am sure they have the best intentions. I don't believe any of the gamblers are interested in this mutilated tree. It would be an act of mercy to release the prisoner and send him back home.

PREVIOUS PAGES: A woman collecting water from a baobab used as a reservoir in the Comoros Islands. The trees were introduced there from Africa hundreds of years ago.
RIGHT: A captive baobab at Sun City close to the Temple of Doom.

ACKNOWLEDGEMENTS

I COULD NOT HAVE WRITTEN THIS BOOK without owing a great
debt to many people all over the world. I also depended on the
kindness of many people in order to take the photographs,
the majority of which are my work.
I should like to mention particularly the following benefactors.
In Madagascar, Suzanne Boigeol, Gertrude Dame, Rolland Ranaivijaona,
David Sayers; in Africa, Mike Amm, Barbara Bailey, Anna and Prospero
Bailey, Nicky and Beesie Bailey, Pam Bowling, Jonathan Bowling, Jessica
and John Clarke, Tana and Dave Hilton-Barber, Jabu Linden, Gail and
Alistair Maytham, Nella Opperman; in Australia, Kingsley Dixon and
Peter Valder; in the Caribbean and Florida, Olasee Davis, Lolly and David
Knight, Fred Krehbiel and Robert Nicholls.
I should like to thank my literary agents, Mike Shaw
and Jonathan Pegg. I should also like to thank the staff of my
London publishers, Weidenfeld & Nicolson, especially my publisher,
Michael Dover; and the staff of my overseas publishers, especially Bob
Weil of Norton in New York and Jonathan Ball of the firm he created in
South Africa. Finally I should like to pay tribute to my long-suffering
family in Ireland, especially my wife Val, who must have sometimes
wondered if my passion for baobabs would ever cool.

BIBLIOGRAPHY

Adanson, Michel, *Familles des Plantes*, 2 vols. Paris 1763-4

Adanson, Michel, *Histoire naturelle de Senegal.* Paris 1757

Adanson, Michel, *A Voyage to Senegal.* (tr.) London 1759

Adanson, Michel, *Histoire de la Botanique* etc, 2nd ed., Paris 1864

Armstrong, P., 'Baobabs – remnants of Gondwanaland?' in *New Scientist*, 73
    pp. 212-3, 1977

Baines, Thomas, *Explorations in South West Africa*, London 1864

Baum, David, 'A systematic revision of Adansonia (Bombacaceae)', in
    Ann. Missouri Bot. Gard., 1995, pp 440-470

Baum, David, 'The comparative pollination and floral biology of baobabs' etc, in
    Ann. Missouri Bot. Gard., 82, 1995, pp 322-48

Cashel, Rowan, *The Baobab in Fact and Fable* (photocopy) London 1995

Chapman, James, *Travels in the Interior of South Africa*, 2 vols, London 1868

Livingstone, David, *Missionary Travels and Researches in South Africa* etc., London 1857

Lowe, Pat, *The Boab Tree*, Port Melbourne, Victoria, 1998

Mshingeni, Keto E. and Hangula, L., *Africa's Baobab Resources* etc. 2001

Palgrave, K.C., *Trees of Southern Africa*, Cape Town, 1977

Palmer, E. and Pitman, N., *Trees of Southern Africa*, 2 vols, Cape Town 1972

Rauh, W. and Herman, Dr. S., *Succulent and Xenophytic Plants of Madagascar*, 2 vols,
    Mill Valley, California, 1995, 1998

Sidibe, M. and Williams, J.T., *Baobab: Adansonia digitata*, L. Southampton
    University, 2002

Simpson, Mark, *The Ecology of the Baobab* etc., London. 1995

Van Wyck, Piet, *Field Guide to the Trees of the Kruger National Park*, Cape Town 1984

Van Wyk, Braam and Van Wyk, Piet, *Field Guide to Trees of Southern Africa*, Cape
    Town, 1997

Wickens, G.E., 'The Baobab – Africa's upside down tree' in *Kew Bulletin*, 37,
    no. 2, 1982

DISTRIBUTION OF BAOBABS

1. WIDESPREAD IN AFRICA*: *Adansonia digitata*.
   (I). CONSIDERED INDIGENOUS: Angola, Benin,
   Botswana, Burkina Faso, Cameroon Cape Verde,
   Chad, Congo, Côte d'Ivoire, Ethiopia, Eritrea,
   Gambia, Ghana, Guinea, Kenya, Malawi, Mali,
   Mauritania, Mozambique, Namibia, Niger, Nigeria,
   Senegal, Sierra Leone, Somalia, South Africa,
   Sudan, Tanzania, Togo, Zambia, Zimbabwe.
   (II). CONSIDERED INTRODUCED: Central African
   Republic, Comoros, Democratic Republic of
   Congo, Egypt, Gabon, Madagascar, São Tomé

2. RESTRICTED TO MADAGASCAR: *Adansonia grandidieri*,
   *A. suarezansis, A. rubrostipa, A. madagascarensis,
   A. za, A. perrieri.*

3. RESTRICTED TO NW AUSTRALIA: *Adansonia gibbosa*.

* Based on a mapping project initiated by Grenville
Lucas, director of the herbarium, Royal Botanic
Gardens, Kew, in 1971 and enlarged by Gerald
Wickens in 1982.

LEFT: A palava tree near Khubu Island, Botswana.
The village elders sit round in its shade.

INDEX

ILLUSTRATION CREDITS

From a Sketch by Captain Henry Need, H.M. Brig Linnet.

Text and photographic copyright
© Thomas Pakenham 2004

First published in Great Britain in 2004.

This edition published in conjunction with Weidenfeld & Nicolson, England in 2004 by JONATHAN BALL PUBLISHERS (PTY) LTD
PO Box 33977
Jeppestown
2043

ISBN 1 86842 201 1

Printed and bound in Italy by Printers, Trento and LEGO, Vicenza.

The text of this book is composed in Village Roman Titling.

Designer: Nigel Soper
Editorial by Claire Wedderburn-Maxwell
Additional Picture Research: Suzanne Bailey

FRONT ENDPAPER: 'Baobabs near bank of Lue' by Thomas Baines.
BACK ENDPAPER: 'Group of Gouty stem trees' by Thomas Baines.